EVERYTHING SPORTS

EVERYTHING SOCCER

DAVID J. CLARKE

SportsZone

An Imprint of Abdo Publishing
abdobooks.com

abdobooks.com

Published by Abdo Publishing, a division of ABDO, PO Box 398166, Minneapolis, Minnesota 55439.

Printed in the United States of America, North Mankato, Minnesota.
052024
092024

THIS BOOK CONTAINS RECYCLED MATERIALS

Cover Photos: Harry How/Getty Images Sport/Getty Images, front (Lionel Messi); Robin Alam/ISI Photos/USSF/Getty Images Sport/Getty Images, front (Sophia Smith); Radu Razvan/Shutterstock Images, front (background), back
Interior Photos: Shaun Botterill/FIFA/Getty Images, 4–5; Rischgitz/Hulton Archive/Getty Images, 6; Alex Pantling/Getty Images Sport/Getty Images, 8–9; Winslow Townson/Getty Images Sport/Getty Images, 11; Mirrorpix/Getty Images, 12–13; Brad Smith/ISI Photos/USSF/Getty Images Sport/Getty Images, 14; Dean Mouhtaropoulos/Getty Images Sport/Getty Images, 15; Alessandro Sabattini/Getty Images Sport/Getty Images, 16–17; Steve Powell/Allsport/Hulton Archive/Getty Images, 19; Quique Garcia/AFP/Getty Images, 21; Doug Pensinger/Allsport/Getty Images Sport/Getty Images, 22–23; David Madison/Getty Images Sport/Getty Images, 24–25; Matt King/Getty Images Sport/Getty Images, 27; David Ramos/Getty Images Sport/Getty Images, 28–29; Juan Manuel Serrano Arce/Getty Images Sport/Getty Images, 31; Matthias Hangst/Getty Images Sport/Getty Images, 32–33, 44–45; Dan Mullan/Getty Images Sport/Getty Images, 34–35; Maddie Meyer/FIFA/Getty Images, 37; Heidtmann/picture alliance/Getty Images, 38–39; AFP/Getty Images, 41; Robert Michael/AFP/Getty Images, 42–43; Mark Leech/Offside/Getty Images, 47; Simon M. Bruty/Anychance/Getty Images Sport/Getty Images, 48–49; Franck Fife/AFP/Getty Images, 50–51; Stu Forster/Getty Images Sport/Getty Images, 52–53; Robert Mora/WireImage/Getty Images, 54; Nick Tre. Smith/Icon Sportswire/Getty Images, 55; Bettmann/Getty Images, 57; Stan Honda/AFP/Getty Images, 58; Alex Grimm/Getty Images Sport/Getty Images, 61

Editor: Patrick Donnelly
Series Designer: Karli Kruse

Library of Congress Control Number: 2023949395
Publisher's Cataloging-in-Publication Data
Names: Clarke, David J., author.
Title: Everything soccer / by David J. Clarke
Description: Minneapolis, Minnesota: Abdo Publishing, 2025 | Series: Everything sports | Includes online resources and index.
Identifiers: ISBN 9781098293604 (lib. bdg.) | ISBN 9798384912873 (ebook)
Subjects: LCSH: Soccer--Juvenile literature. | European football--Juvenile literature. | Soccer players--Juvenile literature. | Soccer teams--Juvenile literature. | Soccer--Clubs--Juvenile literature. | Soccer goalkeepers--Juvenile literature. | Soccer matches--Juvenile literature. | Soccer injuries--Juvenile literature. | Soccer fans--Juvenile literature. | Soccer--Accidents and injuries--Juvenile literature. | Soccer uniforms--Juvenile literature. | Sports--Juvenile literature.
Classification: DDC 796.334--dc23

TABLE OF CONTENTS

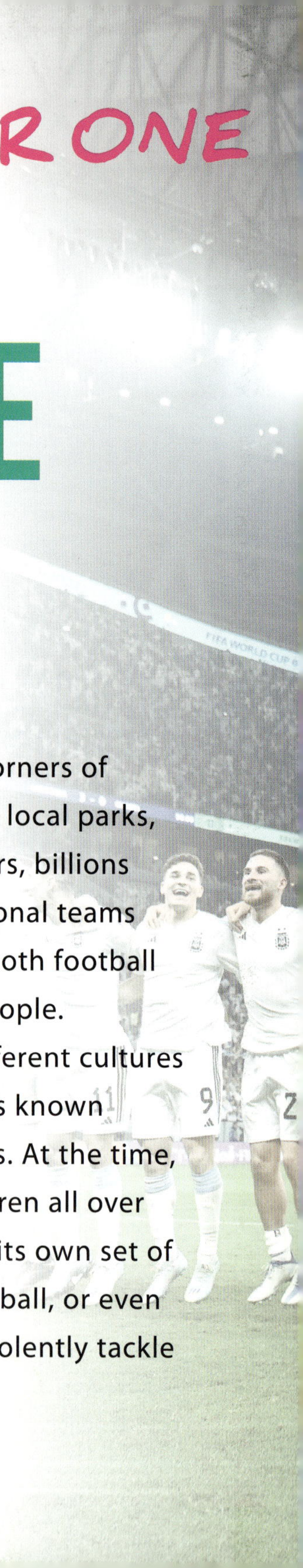

CHAPTER ONE

THE CAMBRIDGE RULES

Today, soccer matches can be found in all corners of the globe. They take place in big stadiums, local parks, beaches, and even city streets. Every four years, billions gather to watch men's and women's international teams fight for the World Cup. The sport known as both football and soccer is practically a religion to many people.

Soccer-like games have been played in different cultures for thousands of years. However, soccer as it is known today developed in England in the early 1800s. At the time, versions of soccer were played by schoolchildren all over the country. But each school seemed to have its own set of rules. In some places, it was OK to handle the ball, or even carry it. Other groups allowed defenders to violently tackle

The 2022 men's World Cup final was considered one of the most exciting soccer matches ever played. Argentina defeated France in a penalty shootout.

Early soccer matches were often disorganized and could be very rough.

opponents, much like modern American football or rugby. No one could decide exactly how many players should be on the field at once.

When these young players got older and went off to college, they found it impossible to agree on how the game should be played. So in the 1840s, students at Cambridge University decided to write down the "official" rules of the sport. By 1848, they had settled on 11 laws of football.

Exactly what they wrote is lost to history. However, 15 years later, a group of clubs in London, England, got together to form the Football Association (FA). The rules they set up for their sport were said to be almost exactly what the Cambridge students had written down. And they laid the foundation of the soccer that fans know today.

For the rest of the 1800s, the sport exploded around England. In 1871, English teams played the first FA Cup. This tournament is still played every year and is open to all English clubs, both professional and amateur. In 1888–89, the English Football League was created to oversee a full season for its member clubs. The league still exists today.

The sport soon spread around Europe. And as Europeans moved around the globe, they took soccer with them. By the early 1900s, countries all over the world had started to develop their

THE CREATION OF FIFA

The Fédération Internationale de Football Association, commonly known as FIFA, was created in 1904. Its goal was to establish global rules for the sport. The organization was mainly founded by European countries, but England was not one of them. England joined FIFA in 1906 but battled with the organization for years over control of soccer. England left FIFA multiple times in the early 1900s. Soccer's founding country didn't permanently join until 1946.

Just under 90,000 fans attended the 2022 men's World Cup final in Qatar. Another 1.5 billion fans watched the match at home.

own leagues and their own passions for soccer. National teams, which featured players representing their home countries, began to play. The 1908 Olympics in London featured one of the first major international tournaments.

As soccer spread around the world, different countries and regions developed their own styles of play. England has always been known for its physical game. Italy developed cautious, defensive tactics. South American countries such as Brazil and Argentina are famous for their passion and offensive flair. No matter how it is played, soccer continues as the world's favorite sport.

CHAPTER TWO

BOOTS AND THE BALL

Soccer doesn't require a lot of equipment. But it can't be played without a ball. Through the centuries, soccer balls have been made of rubber, leather, and synthetic materials. Ancient balls were often made of animal skins. People who can't afford to buy a ball have been known to play with rolled up socks or shirts.

For much of soccer's early years, official game balls were made of rubber bladders covered in leather. They were heavy and got even heavier when they became wet. By the end of a match in the rain, kicking the ball was like smacking a boulder.

Synthetic balls didn't exist until the 1960s. At the same time, the balls started to have a new look. Early balls had been made of either eight or 18 individual panels sewn together. The 32-panel ball debuted in the 1960s. It was a series of 20 hexagons and 12 pentagons. Most balls since have been made in that style.

Soccer shoes and balls have gone through many changes during the modern history of the sport.

An Italian player chases the famous Telstar ball at the 1970 World Cup in Mexico.

The most iconic 32-panel ball debuted at the 1970 men's World Cup. That year, Adidas was asked to design the official ball for the tournament. The company created the Telstar. The ball had a simple design of white hexagons and black pentagons. It was used again for the 1974 men's tournament in West Germany. Adidas has made the balls at every World Cup since. Every four years, the company creates a new design inspired by the host country.

Just like balls, soccer shoes (also called "boots") have evolved over the years. Early shoes were made of leather and looked like high-top work boots. Cleats didn't exist, so players screwed metal tacks into the soles for better traction. Like the leather balls, these boots were heavy. Even worse, some of them also had metal toe caps. Getting kicked was very painful.

The metal caps and tacks were eventually removed,

THE JABULANI

The most controversial ball in World Cup history was used for the 2010 men's tournament in South Africa. That year, Adidas developed the Jabulani. The name came from a Zulu word meaning "celebrate." But few players were happy with the ball. It was made from only eight panels and was closer to a perfect sphere than any ball used before. Its shape caused it to dip and swerve unpredictably. One Brazilian striker called it "supernatural." Goalkeepers hated it, and even outfield players had trouble controlling their shots and long passes.

but it wasn't until the 1960s that soccer shoes began to look like today's models. Companies such as Adidas and Puma were some of the first to create synthetic shoes, which were lighter. They also handled water better.

Legendary Brazilian star Pelé made Puma shoes famous when he wore the company's "King" style boots at the

Megan Rapinoe wore these boots to celebrate her 200th appearance for the US Women's National Team.

The name of Adidas's Copa Mundial boot comes from the Spanish translation for World Cup.

1970 World Cup. It wasn't long before all the top players had their favorite shoes. And the companies liked having players market them. The most famous shoe of all is Adidas's Copa Mundial. The simple black shoe with the company's white, three-striped logo debuted in 1979. Over the years, top stars including Franz Beckenbauer, Diego Maradona, David Beckham, and Zinédine Zidane have worn them. The shoe is thought to be the all-time top seller.

CHAPTER THREE

LEGENDARY MEN

For decades, fans have debated who is the best men's player of all time. What side of the argument a person lands on often depends on where they are from. An English fan might point to Sir Bobby Charlton. The midfielder led England to its only World Cup win in 1966 with his thundering long-range shots. French fans champion Zinédine Zidane, who scored twice in the 1998 World Cup final held in Paris as France beat Brazil 3–0.

Others in France might opt for Kylian Mbappé, the speedster who helped his nation win again in 2018 and had a hat trick in the 2022 final. German fans might counter with Franz Beckenbauer. "Der Kaiser" revolutionized the sport in the 1970s by attacking from his defensive position. At the same time, Dutch forward Johan Cruyff dazzled onlookers with his silky skills.

Pelé scored 77 goals in 92 appearances for the Brazilian national team.

Around the world, there are other legends such as Lev Yashin of the former Soviet Union. In 1962, he became the only goalkeeper to ever win the Ballon d'Or award, given to the best player in Europe at the time. George Weah of Liberia won that award in 1995, after it was opened up to players from the rest of the world. He is just one of many African superstars to make their mark on the game. Asia, too, has icons, such as strikers Ali Daei of Iran and Son Heung-Min of South Korea.

However, any list of the very best men's players likely includes only four names. When Pelé passed away in December 2022, tributes poured in from all over the world for the Brazilian. At 17 years old, he made a splash by leading Brazil to its first World Cup victory. He scored twice in that 1958 final as Brazil won 5–2. Over the next 20 years, he thrilled the world with his goal scoring and flair. He led Brazil to World Cup glory again in 1962 and a third time in 1970.

Argentina is Brazil's main soccer rival, and the country boasts two stars that are also discussed as the best. Diego Maradona stood only 5 feet, 5 inches tall, but he played like a giant. The midfielder had speed, quickness, and jaw-dropping dribbling ability. His personal life was controversial, but he was worshiped in his home country.

A decade after Maradona retired, another short Argentinian burst onto the scene. Five-foot, seven-inch Lionel Messi first impressed fans as a teenager with top

Diego Maradona scored five goals and added five assists for Argentina at the 1986 World Cup.

Spanish club Barcelona. He was soon smashing goal-scoring records with his quick feet and deft shooting touch. For years, he struggled to have the same success with Argentina's national team. That changed at the 2022 World Cup in Qatar. Messi scored seven goals in the tournament and assisted on three more. He guided Argentina to its first title since Maradona led the nation to victory in 1986.

Messi's chief rival in the 2000s and 2010s was Cristiano Ronaldo. The Portuguese winger spent many years with Barcelona's top opponent, Real Madrid. Each match between the rival clubs is called "*El Clásico*." And the spectacle of the two best players on the field together made fans take notice of these games. Ronaldo's powerful sprinting stride made him tough to stop. He could also score goals with his head and was an excellent free-kick taker. In September 2021, he became the highest

WHO SCORED THE MOST

Because soccer players compete in so many matches in different competitions, counting their goals can be tricky. The debate rages over who has the most goals of all time. Both Cristiano Ronaldo and Lionel Messi have more than 800 career goals. Officially, Pelé has 769, though some credit him with more than 1,200. Critics say that total can be reached only by including the Brazilian's goals from matches that weren't official.

Lionel Messi (10) and Cristiano Ronaldo played against each other 36 times in their careers.

scorer of all-time in men's international play when he notched his 110th goal for Portugal in a win over Ireland.

CHAPTER FOUR

LEGENDARY WOMEN

For most of the 1900s, women were discouraged from playing soccer. Many countries even banned the sport. But since women's soccer started to grow in the 1980s, some women have wasted no time in reaching legendary status.

Many of the sport's first female stars were American. Michelle Akers joined the US Women's National Team (USWNT) when it was formed in 1985. By 1991, the forward was leading her country to victory in what would later be known as the first Women's World Cup. And while Akers was a great scorer, she was also versatile. Later in her career she became a standout defensive midfielder.

In the late 1980s five future superstars joined the USWNT. Defender Kristine Lilly first played for the national team in 1987. By the time she retired in 2010, she had a record

Michelle Akers was named the co-Player of the Century in 2000. She shared the award with Chinese star Sun Wen.

354 appearances. Joy Fawcett was a star scorer in college at the University of California. With the national team she became a stalwart defender. Julie Foudy directed the team from her attacking midfield position. Brandi Chastain was another standout on defense. Her penalty shootout goal to win the 1999 World Cup final at the Rose Bowl in California still stands as one of soccer's most famous moments.

The biggest star to emerge from the Fab Five was Mia Hamm. The striker retired in 2004 with a then-record 158 international goals. Hamm also paved the way for women to become celebrity athletes. The humble superstar was highly sought after for commercials and endorsements.

Hamm's record was eventually broken by another USWNT legend, Abby Wambach. The Rochester, New York, native finished her career in 2015 with 184 international goals. Many of those were set up by winger Megan Rapinoe, who

SINCLAIR THE SNIPER

On January 29, 2020, a Canadian striker ripped the women's international goal-scoring record out of the hands of American stars. Christine Sinclair scored twice against St. Kitts and Nevis that day. They were her 184th and 185th international goals. Sinclair retired from international soccer in 2023 with 190 career goals.

Mia Hamm played in four World Cups for the United States between 1991 and 2003.

helped the United States win two World Cups before retiring in 2023.

As the sport has grown, the list of stars from around the world has as well. In the 1990s, Chinese striker Sun Wen was admired by players everywhere for her all-around skill. Germany's Birgit Prinz helped her country win six major international tournaments, including back-to-back World Cups in 2003 and 2007. At the 2003 tournament, Prinz led all scorers with seven goals. In 2007, Prinz's teammate Nadine Angerer became the only goalkeeper to ever post six shutouts in a World Cup. Brazilian legend Marta also made her first World Cup appearance in 2003. The dazzling striker became the first player, male or female, to appear in six World Cups when she played in the 2023 tournament at 37 years old. She also holds the tournament's record with 17 career goals.

Homare Sawa was the inspirational leader behind Japan's dramatic World Cup victory in 2011. Her goal in extra time against the United States tied the match. Japan won on penalties. By that time, the 32-year-old midfielder had been a national team player for 18 years.

Though many legends have left the women's game in recent years, a new generation is ready to step up. Powerful defender Wendie Renard has helped turn France into an

Australian star Sam Kerr celebrates after scoring against New Zealand during a match in 2022.

international powerhouse. She teamed up with Norwegian scorer Ada Hegerberg on France's best club team, Lyon. Australian forward Sam Kerr nearly helped her underdog nation on a run to the final at the 2023 tournament held in her home country. That tournament was won by Spain, which boasted superstar Aitana Bonmatí. The midfielder was named the Golden Ball winner as the World Cup's best player after scoring three goals and adding two assists.

CHAPTER FIVE

BUILDING A CLUB

Teams in American sports leagues often are formed the same way. Wealthy owners pay a fee to enter an existing league, and they start a team in a certain city. Most men's soccer clubs around the world began much more organically. Many English clubs started as factory teams. For example, London club West Ham United's first players were employees at an ironworks. The team is still nicknamed the "Irons."

Many clubs around the world were either started or influenced by English people living abroad. An Englishman named Herbert Kilpin founded AC Milan, one of the most successful teams in Italy. Clubs that copy such English team names as Everton and Arsenal show up in several other countries.

Many professional clubs around the world, including top teams like Real Madrid, are owned by the club's members.

No matter how they started, certain clubs have grown to represent specific groups. Some cities have one club for working-class fans and another aligned with more affluent people. In Scotland, the two biggest clubs are Celtic and Rangers. Both play in Glasgow. Rangers are known as the team of protestants, while Celtic represents the city's Catholics. At times, that religious divide has caused problems, including violence, at matches.

HOLLYWOOD IN WALES

In 2020, actors Rob McElhenney and Ryan Reynolds bought Wrexham FC, located in Wales. The club was struggling in the fifth level of English soccer at the time. Wrexham was founded in 1864, making it one of the oldest clubs in the world. But not many fans outside of the region knew about it. That changed when the new owners' efforts to turn the team around were turned into a popular television show, *Welcome to Wrexham*.

In 2005, English club Manchester United was bought by American owners. The sale upset some local fans. They decided to quit rooting for Manchester United and instead start their own team. FC United of Manchester was born. One of the club's other proposed names was Newton Heath United. It was a nod to the original name of Manchester United. The famous team was founded as Newton Heath LYR Football Club in 1878.

One club with a unique structure is Athletic Bilbao of Spain. Bilbao is a city in the country's Basque region, near France. The proud people there have long wished to have their own country. Bilbao celebrates that by signing only Basque players. Spain's top division was founded in 1929. Despite limiting its talent pool to a region of just under 2.2 million people, Bilbao has never been relegated. The team has even won the league eight times.

Local stars such as Iñaki Williams take great pride in playing for Athletic Bilbao.

CHAPTER SIX

THE WORLD CUPS

By 1930, men's soccer had been played in the Olympics for more than two decades. But FIFA wanted to hold its own tournament. That's how the World Cup was born. The first men's World Cup was held in Uruguay. Only 13 teams played. Many European nations decided it was too expensive to travel to South America. The host country beat Argentina 4–2 in the final.

By the 1950s, the tournament had grown into one of the most popular sporting events in the world. It was a 16-team tournament until 1982. That year it grew to 24 teams. The 1998 tournament in France was the first to feature 32 teams. In 2017, FIFA announced that the 2026 tournament will have 48 teams.

French star Kylian Mbappé kisses the World Cup trophy after France defeated Croatia 4–2 at the 2018 men's World Cup in Russia.

Through the years, 80 countries have played in the men's World Cup. However, only eight have won it. Brazil leads the way with five victories. The nation's 1970 championship team featured several stars, including Pelé. Many consider that year's squad the best international team ever. Italy has four titles. The Italians were also the first country to win back-to-back World Cups. They did so in 1934 and 1938.

Between 1949 and 1990 Germany was split into separate countries, West Germany and East Germany. West Germany won the World Cup three times. The country was then reunited. It won again in 2014. Argentina captured its third World Cup in 2022. France and Uruguay have each won twice. England and Spain have one victory apiece.

The Women's World Cup didn't begin until 1991.

TRULY A WORLD CUP

The men's World Cup has traditionally been hosted by one country. In 2002, Japan and South Korea combined as hosts. FIFA awarded the 2026 tournament to three countries—Canada, Mexico, and the United States. The 2030 tournament marks the men's World Cup's 100th anniversary. It will be a global event. Most of the tournament will take place in Morocco, Portugal, and Spain. But the first match is scheduled to be played in Uruguay as a tribute to the 1930 tournament. Paraguay and Argentina were also named as hosts for one match each.

Lionel Messi scored twice in the final to lead Argentina to victory at the 2022 men's World Cup in Qatar.

The first tournament was played in China. It wasn't even called the World Cup. FIFA wasn't sure a women's tournament would catch on, so it didn't use the name. The United States won that year. Eight years later, the Americans beat China in a penalty shootout to win again. The game was played in front of 90,185 fans at the Rose Bowl in Southern California. At the time, that was a record for a women's sporting event.

The United States added its third and fourth titles in 2015 and 2019. Germany took home back-to-back championships in 2003 and 2007. Japan outlasted the United States for its first title in 2011. Norway also has one title, which came in 1995. Spain won its first in 2023.

The Women's World Cup continues to grow. The 2023 tournament was played in New Zealand and Australia. It was the first to feature 32 teams. Nearly 2 million fans attended games to set a record.

Spain became the fifth country to win a Women's World Cup by beating England 1–0 in the 2023 final.

CHAPTER SEVEN

LEGENDARY GOALS

There are few moments in sports quite like the instant a soccer goal is scored. The ball goes in the net, and the stadium rocks as joyous fans celebrate. Players skid and slide all over the turf as they perform creative celebrations.

Certain goals, however, live on for many reasons. In the 1970 men's World Cup final, Brazilian forward Tostão won the ball from an Italian player. What happened next is often called the best display of teamwork ever seen on a soccer field. As Brazil advanced forward, eight of the team's 10 outfield players touched the ball. Some players weaved past defenders with creative dribbles. Others played pinpoint passes. The ball ended up with Pelé at the edge of the Italian penalty area. He was facing the goal. But instead of shooting, Pelé played a no-look pass to an open space

Brazilian forwards Pelé (10) and Tostão (9) race behind the net to celebrate Carlos Alberto's famous goal against Italy in the 1970 men's World Cup final.

HAT TRICK HEROES

Scoring a hat trick in a match is a difficult task. But three players have done it in soccer's biggest game—the World Cup final. England's Geoff Hurst was the first to do it, in 1966. Two of his three goals against West Germany came in extra time of a 4–2 England win. In 2015, Carli Lloyd of the United States scored three in a 5–2 final win over Japan. One of them was a lob from the halfway line. France's Kylian Mbappé matched the feat against Argentina in the 2022 men's final. Mbappé also converted a penalty kick in the shootout, but France lost the match.

on his right. Defender Carlos Alberto was sprinting into that area. He took the pass in stride and thundered a shot into the Italian net. The brilliant move capped off Brazil's 4–1 win. The goal is still seen as proof by some that the 1970 Brazilian team was the greatest team ever.

Other goals are remembered because they show off a player's individual skills. In the quarterfinals of the 1986 men's World Cup, Argentina was playing England. Early in the second half, Argentina's superstar Diego Maradona collected a pass in midfield. He charged forward, sprinting past English defenders with the ball seemingly glued to his feet. Even when some English players tried to foul him, Maradona kept going. He eventually broke past everyone before beating the goalkeeper with a low shot. The magic moment was eventually nicknamed the "Goal of the Century." Earlier in

Diego Maradona (10) dribbles past two English defenders on his way to the Goal of the Century in the 1986 World Cup quarterfinal against England.

the game, Maradona had scored another memorable goal. This one was controversial, as it appeared to deflect off his hand and into the net. Maradona later said "the hand of God" helped guide the ball. The two goals lifted Argentina to a 2–1 victory.

Other goals live on because they came late in important matches. The United States trailed Brazil 2–1 during the quarterfinals of the 2011 Women's World Cup. To make matters worse, the Americans had only 10 players on the field. Defender Rachel Buehler had earned a red card in the second half, meaning the United States had to play the rest of the game one player short.

The game reached the 122nd minute, and there were likely only seconds left to play. American winger Megan Rapinoe had the ball on the left sideline. She hoisted a long, looping cross to the far side of the Brazilian goal. Forward Abby Wambach charged in, outjumping a defender and the Brazilian goalkeeper. Wambach powered a header into the net to tie the game. It was the latest goal ever scored in a men's or women's World Cup match. The United States eventually won in a penalty shootout.

Abby Wambach's goal against Brazil was one of 14 she scored in four Women's World Cups during her career.

CHAPTER EIGHT

THE PENALTY SPOT

The 120 thrilling minutes of regulation and extra-time play at the 2022 men's World Cup final in Qatar had settled nothing. Argentina and France were still tied 3–3. What many considered to be the greatest World Cup final in history was to be decided on a penalty shootout.

Not everyone loves seeing penalty shootouts. While they are filled with tension and drama, some fans see them as a poor way to decide a match. In a sport known for its flowing beauty, these fans hate that a game comes down to free shots from 12 yards (11 m) away.

However, penalty shootouts bring fans to the edges of their seats. That was certainly true in the 2022 final. And they can make heroes out of unlikely players. In Qatar, Argentina was led by Lionel Messi and France by Kylian Mbappé, two global superstars. But both shot early in the shootout. Each scored, which left it up to other players to finish it off.

France's Kylian Mbappé (10) beats Argentina goalkeeper Emiliano Martínez with a penalty kick in the 2022 World Cup final.

It was little-known right back Gonzalo Montiel who hit the deciding kick to win the World Cup for Argentina.

On the other hand, a penalty shootout failure can tarnish a player's legacy. The 1994 men's World Cup final between Brazil and Italy went to a shootout. Italy's best player, Roberto Baggio, stepped up needing to score to prevent a Brazilian victory. Many Italian fans will never forget the moment Baggio hammered his shot high over the bar.

PENALTY ACES

Some countries have developed reputations for being better at penalty shootouts than others. West Germany/Germany has famously never lost a penalty shootout in men's World Cup play. Gary Lineker was on the England team that was knocked out in a shootout by West Germany in the 1990 World Cup semifinals. After the match, Lineker famously said, "Football is a simple game—22 men chase a ball around for 90 minutes and at the end, the Germans always win."

The pressure is all on the shooter. That's because they are expected to score. Roughly 75 percent of penalty kicks go in. Stopping one during a game can kick off a wild celebration. In the 2019 Women's World Cup semifinals, American goalkeeper Alyssa Naeher stuffed England captain Steph Houghton's second-half penalty. The save preserved a 2–1 lead for the USWNT. As Naeher held the ball, the rest of the US players surrounded her in a

Italy's Roberto Baggio led his country to the World Cup final in 1994, but his missed penalty sealed Brazil's win.

Germany's Jens Lehmann stretches to stop a penalty against Argentina at the 2006 World Cup. Lehmann's penalty "cheat sheet" was later auctioned off for $1.3 million, which went to charity.

joyous group hug. Naeher had to remind her teammates that the game was still going on.

Goalkeepers try all sorts of tricks to gain an edge. In the 2022 men's World Cup final, Argentina goalkeeper Emiliano Martínez tried several strange tactics to distract French shooters. He tossed the ball away from one player. Then he smiled at another. Eventually the referee gave Martínez a yellow card. But the plan seemed to work. Two rattled French shooters missed.

Germany and Argentina were locked in a tense shootout at the men's World Cup in 2006. But German goalkeeper Jens Lehmann had a secret weapon. Before each shooter, Lehmann pulled a crumpled piece of paper out of one of his socks and looked it over. It was a sheet that noted where each Argentine player liked to aim. Lehmann stopped two shots and Germany won.

CHAPTER NINE

SOCCER'S DYNASTIES

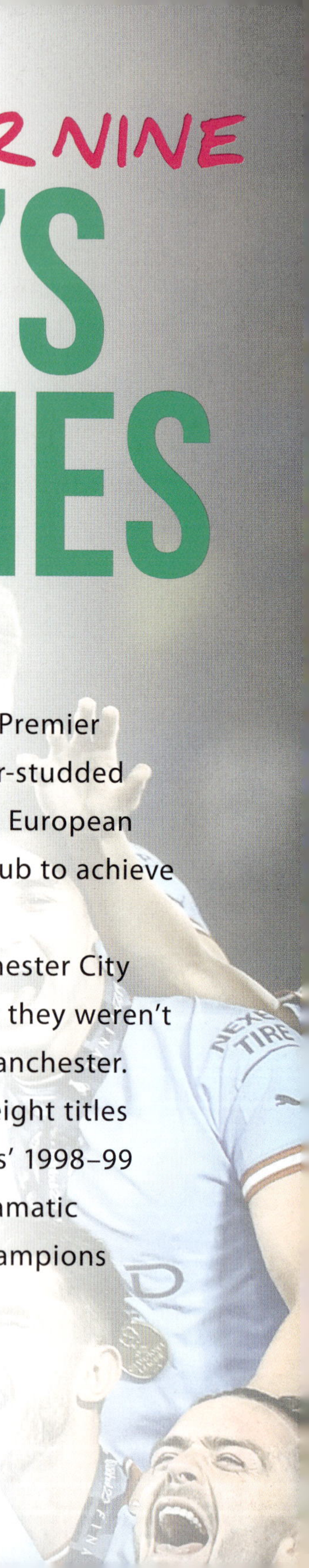

In 2022–23, Manchester City won the English Premier League for the fifth time in six years. The star-studded team also won England's FA Cup as well as the European Champions League. That made City the rare club to achieve what is known in soccer as a "treble."

Many fans started wondering where Manchester City ranked among soccer's greatest dynasties. But they weren't even the first Premier League dynasty from Manchester. City's rivals, Manchester United, had claimed eight titles between 1992–93 and 2002–03. The Red Devils' 1998–99 season came with a treble, capped off by a dramatic win over Bayern Munich of Germany in the Champions League final.

Manchester City players celebrate on the field after beating Inter Milan 1–0 to win the 2023 men's European Champions League final.

Bayern Munich might have lost that match. But the German club has long dominated the country's top league, the Bundesliga. The league was founded in 1963. Bayern Munich won its 32nd title in 2022–23. No other German team had more than five in that span.

Other countries have multiple men's dynasty clubs. In Spain, La Liga has been historically dominated by Real Madrid and FC Barcelona. In Italy, Juventus of Turin had won 36 championships through 2023, while both Inter Milan and AC Milan had won 19. Scottish rivals Rangers and Celtic have won over 100 league titles between them. The rest of the country's clubs have 19 combined wins.

AL AHLY

Soccer clubs measure success in trophies, whether they are in league or cup competitions. By that score, no team comes close to Al Ahly, the top men's club in Egypt. The Cairo-based team won the Egyptian league, Egyptian Super Cup, and African Champions League in 2022–23. That brought its trophy total to 149 since the club was founded in 1907. No other team in the world had more than 115.

Major League Soccer (MLS) has never seen any team dominate to that level. But that does not mean there haven't been dynasty clubs. DC United won the first MLS Cup in 1996 against LA Galaxy on an overtime header by defender Eddie Pope. That set in motion the first MLS dynasty. DC United won two

Matches between Rangers (in blue) and Celtic are often heated and controversial.

more titles in the next three years. In the 2000s, one club maintained a mini dynasty despite switching cities. The San Jose Earthquakes won the MLS Cup for the first time in 2003. By 2006 the franchise had moved to Houston to become the Dynamo. It won titles in each of its first two seasons in Texas.

However, no MLS club has won more titles than LA Galaxy. The club won its first in 2002, then again in 2005. But Los Angeles' best run came from 2011 to 2014. Led by star American midfielder Landon Donovan, the Galaxy won three titles in four years.

The Portland Thorns rose above the pack in the first 10 seasons of the National Women's Soccer League (NWSL). The club won three league titles in four championship appearances. But the Thorns have a long way to go to catch Europe's top women's dynasties. Barcelona's women won La Liga Femenina eight times between 2012 and 2023.

Landon Donovan scored the winning goal in both the 2011 and 2012 MLS Cup finals for LA Galaxy.

Portland Thorns striker Sophia Smith (9) is congratulated by teammates after scoring in the fourth minute of the 2022 NWSL Cup final against Kansas City Current. Portland won the match 2–0.

Between 2007 and 2023, French club Lyon won all but one of the Division I Fémenine's championships. Both of those clubs also dominated in the European Champions League. Between 2016 and 2023, Lyon won the competition six times. Barcelona won the other two.

CHAPTER TEN

SOCCER IN AMERICA

In 1930, the US Men's National Team traveled to Uruguay for the first World Cup. The team finished third out of 13 teams, but few people in the United States noticed. The same was true 20 years later. The Americans famously upset world power England by a 1–0 score at the 1950 World Cup. The *New York Times* didn't believe the result was real. The paper didn't even mention the game. And the US team didn't go back to another World Cup for 40 years. Women's soccer, meanwhile, was still decades away.

For most of the 1900s, American soccer struggled just to gain respect. Most Americans wanted to watch American football, baseball, and basketball instead. In 1968, the United States finally formed a professional league that had some staying power. The North American Soccer League (NASL) at one point had 24 teams. The best was the New York Cosmos. The club attracted international superstars such as Franz Beckenbauer and Pelé. The Cosmos regularly played for crowds of 40,000, and they won five league titles.

Despite the Cosmos' period of success, the NASL ran out of money and folded in 1985. Later in the decade, the United States was awarded the 1994 men's World Cup. FIFA's only ask was that a new men's league be formed. Because of

Pelé played just 64 matches for the New York Cosmos but scored 37 times.

David Beckham's arrival in MLS in 2007 signaled a new era for the league.

that, MLS first played in 1996. It wasn't an immediate hit. The league nearly folded in the early 2000s. But slowly, MLS began to grow. In 2007, English superstar David Beckham joined LA Galaxy. His move helped show that MLS was serious about becoming a top league. By 2023, MLS had grown from its original 10 teams to 29. A 30th team was planned for the 2025 season.

The men's national team hoped to grow as well. And while the US men had made progress, the furthest they got in eight World Cups from 1990 to 2022 was the quarterfinals. But with top players such as Christian Pulisic and Weston McKennie now playing in Europe's best leagues, there is plenty of hope for the future.

On the women's side, the United States didn't even have a national team until 1985. But the USWNT grew quickly. Led by top college coach Anson Dorrance, the USWNT won the first Women's World Cup in 1991. Eight years later, the tournament was held in the United States. Record crowds showed that women's soccer had an audience.

The USWNT's title in 1999 showcased a team that was setting a standard

YOUTH SOCCER BOOM

In 1969, only around 49,000 high schoolers were playing soccer in the United States. By the time the United States hosted the 1994 World Cup, that number was up to 421,000. That made it the fifth most popular high school sport in the country. In 2022, soccer's participation had doubled again to 828,000 high school players. That was slightly higher than baseball and softball combined. Only track and field, American football, and basketball had more participants at the prep level.

for greatness both on and off the pitch. The US women thrived early on with a reputation for their work ethic and athleticism. But as the sport has grown and has become more technical, new players such as Naomi Girma and Sophia Smith are working to keep the USWNT among the best of the best.

Starting a league was trickier for American women. Three leagues were started in the late 1990s and early 2000s, but none made it past a third season. A fourth lasted from 2009 to 2012. But the next year the NWSL opened with eight teams. The league got a huge boost when the USWNT won the World Cup in 2015 and again in 2019. Fans started coming back to the women's game. The NWSL completed its 10th season in 2023. Three of its now 12 teams averaged more than 18,000 fans per game.

The USWNT won four of the first eight Women's World Cup tournaments.

GLOSSARY

amateur

A person who plays a sport without getting paid.

club

The team a player competes with outside of his or her national team.

dynasty

A team that has an extended period of success, usually winning multiple championships in the process.

evolve

To grow or change.

hat trick

Three or more goals by the same player in one game.

header

A shot or pass that involves striking the ball with one's head.

iconic

Well known for excellence.

relegated

When a team is demoted from a higher league to a lower league.

rival

An opponent with whom a player or team has a fierce and ongoing competition.

synthetic

Manufactured, not natural.

treble

Winning three major trophies in one season.

versatile

Able to perform many different roles or functions.

yellow card

A caution given to a player by a referee for playing dangerously or behaving badly.

MORE INFORMATION

Books

Clarke, David J. *Soccer Strategies*. Abdo, 2024.

Hewson, Anthony K. *GOATs of Soccer*. Abdo, 2022.

Marthaler, Jon. *The Best Teams of World Soccer*. Abdo, 2024.

Online Resources

Booklinks
NONFICTION NETWORK
FREE! ONLINE NONFICTION RESOURCES

To learn more about soccer, please visit **abdobooklinks.com** or scan this QR code. These links are routinely monitored and updated to provide the most current information available.

INDEX

About the Author

David J. Clarke is a freelance sportswriter. Originally from Helena, Montana, he now lives in Savannah, Georgia, with his golden retriever, Gus.